A B C

Abecedarium Latinum

Primi Gradus in Latinitatem

Peter Sipes
Illustrations: Jessica Rojas

Pluteo Pleno • Crystal Lake, Illinois

Abecedarium Latinum
Primi Gradus in Latinitatem

Peter Sipes
Illustrations: Jessica Rojas

Pluteo Pleno
61 West Woodstock Street
Crystal Lake, Illinois 60014

www.pluteopleno.com

For my mother, Cheryl Sipes, who taught me the alphabet.

Edition 1.0, 2011

Paperback ISBN 978-1-937847-00-5
eBook ISBN 978-1-937847-01-2

Līterae Latīnae

Aa	ā
Bb	bē
Cc	cē
Dd	dē
Ee	ē
Ff	ef
Gg	gē
Hh	hā
Ii	ī vōcālis
Ii	ī cōnsonans
Kk	kā
Ll	el
Mm	em
Nn	en
Oo	ō
Pp	pē
Qq	cū
Rr	er
Ss	es
Tt	tē
Uu	ū
Vv	ū cōnsonans
Xx	ix
Yy	ipsīlon
Zz	zēta

A

apis

Alia verba quae A incipiuntur

auris • autumnus • aestas • anulus • arbor
avis • āeroplanum • armarium

B

bubō

Alia verba quae B incipiuntur

banāna • bracae • basium • birota
brachium • balneum • barba

C

canis

Alia verba quae C incipiuntur

cāseus • cereālia • cēna • crustulum
clāvis • castellum • crūs • cista

D

dracō

Alia verba quae D incipiuntur

domus • dinosaurus • diēs • digitus
discus • dēns • donum

E

elephantus

Alia verba quae E incipiuntur

eruca • esculentum • equus • ēmptor
ecclēsia • eques • effigiēs

F

fulmen

Alia verba quae F incipiuntur

fundus • furnus • faciēs • folium
fenestra • ferculum • furca • flōs

G

gryphus

Alia verba quae G incipiuntur

genū • gutta • gēns • grex • grāmen
glaciēs • gigas

H

hōrologium

Alia verba quae H incipiuntur

harēna • herba • hortus • hiems • holus

ignis

Alia verba quae I vōcālī incipiuntur

īnsula • imber • ignis • impedīmenta
instrūmentum

I

Iuppiter

Alia verba quae I cōnsonantī incipiuntur

iēntāculum • iūs • iānua

K

kalendae

Nūlla alia verba k incipiuntur.

L

lūna

Alia verba quae L incipiuntur

liber • lac • lūdus • lectus • lactūca
later • lacus • lītus • littera • lagoena

M

mūs

Alia verba quae M incipiuntur

mulier • mālum • manus • mōns
macellum • malleus • mare

N

nāvis

Alia verba quae N incipiuntur

nāsus • nūbes • nix • nauta • naufragium
nōdus • nummus • numerus

O

ovis

Alia verba quae O incipiuntur

ōs • ōlla • oculus • ōstium •ōsculum
ōrnāmentum

17

P

pāpiliō

Alia verba quae P incipiuntur

prandium • pirum • puer • puella • pānis
porcus • pila • pōculum • pupa • pēs • pōns

quisquiliae

Alia verba quae Q incipiuntur

quārta pars • quidnam!?

R

rāna

Alia verba quae R incipiuntur

rīsus • raeda • rēmigium • rēx • rēgīna
rixa • rēte

sīmia

Alia verba quae S incipiuntur

sōl • senex • sandal • scala • saccus • scālae
sarcina • specilia • solānum

T

taurus

Alia verba quae T incipiuntur

tempus • tramen • tractor • theātrum
tabulātum • tēlephōnum • turris • tuba

U

ursus

Alia verba quae U incipiuntur

ūva • umbella • umerum

V

vespertiliō

Alia verba quae V incipiuntur

vir • vēr • via • vēndor • ventus • versipellis

X

xiphiās

Nūlla alia verba X incipiuntur.

X

xiphiās

Nūlla alia verba X incipiuntur.

Y

Nūlla verba Y incipiuntur.

Pauper ipsīlon.

zebra

Alia verba quae Z incipiuntur

zōna

For parents

I don't really expect that you know Latin. But over the last several years, you've been asking me what resources are available for the youngest students of Latin. That's why you have this book.

Here are some resources to help you use this book with your children.

Phrases in this book

Alia verba quae Z incipiuntur
Other words which are started with Z.

Nūlla alia verba quae X incipiuntur.
No other words are started with X.

Nūlla verba Y incipiuntur.
No words are started with Y.

Pauper ipsīlon.
Poor Y.

Every other word is found in the glossary on p. 30

Recordings in two pronunciations
Classical: www.pluteopleno.com/downloads/abecedarium_classical.mp3
Ecclesiastical: www.pluteopleno.com/downloads/abecedarium_ecclesiastical.mp3

Activity ideas
www.pluteopleno.com/downloads/abecedarium_ideas.pdf
Have a cool idea to add to it? I'll update this page with the best.

General information
Website: www.pluteopleno.com
Facebook: www.facebook.com/pages/Pluteo-Pleno/203699121404
YouTube: www.youtube.com/user/PluteoPleno

Pronunciation Guide

Two bits of good news: first, you already know the alphabet, and Latin is a phonetic language. So you pronounce it like it's written. Many, but not all, of the sounds that letters make are also going to be very familiar to you. Some will be quite different.

Consonants

All are like English consonants except:
c: always like the *c* in car
g: always like the *g* in gold
i: (when a consonant) like *y* in yet
q: always with *u*, like English
r: rolled like Spanish and Italian
s: always like *s* in snake
t: like *t* in top
v: like *w*
x: always like *x* in ax
z: like the *ds* like in fads

Consonant combinations

bs: like *ps* in tops
bt: like *pt* in apt
ch: like the *ck-h* in knock hard
gn: like *ni* in onion
ph: like the *p-h* in top hat
th: like the *t-h* in hot head

Double consonants

Pronounce each consonant. For example, the words *sumus* (we are) and *summus* (highest) sound different because one has one m and the other has two.

Vowels

a: like *o* in shot
ā: like *a* in father
e: like *e* in bet
ē: like *ay* in day
i: like *i* in in
ī: like *i* in machine
o: like the *o* in no
ō: like the *ow* in row
u: like *u* in dude
ū: like *oo* in food
y: say Latin *e* while holding your lips like Latin *u* (tricky)
ȳ: like Latin *y* but a bit longer

Diphthongs

Vowels in combination
ae: like the English word I
au: like the English word ow
ei: like the *ay* in hay
eu: tricky, like hey you without the *h* and *y*
oe: like the *oi* in oil
ui: like the *ooey* in gooey

Word stress

See glossarium (next page) for where the stress goes.

You stress

If you still don't feel comfortable, cheat. Spanish is really close. Use its pronunciation.

Glossarium

Every word in this book is listed along with its definition. In addition to this, the genitive case, declension and gender are given for a more complete picture. Stress is indicated with bold type.

A

āe**ro**planum, āe**ro**planī – 2n – airplane
aestas, aes**tā**tis – 3f – summer
anulus, **a**nulī – 2m – ring
apis, apis – 3If – bee
arbor, **ar**boris – 3f – tree
ar**ma**rium, ar**ma**riī – 2n – cabinet
auris, **au**ris – 3If – ear
au**tum**nus, au**tum**nī – 2m – fall
avis, **a**vis – 3If – bird

B

balneum, **bal**neī – 2n – bath
ba**nā**na, ba**nā**nae – 1f – banana
barba, barbae – 1f – beard
basium, basiī – 2n – kiss
birota, **bi**rotae – 1f – bicycle
bracae, bracārum – 1f – pants
brachium, **bra**chiī – 2n – arm
bubō, bu**bō**nis – 3f – owl

C

canis, **ca**nis – 3Im, 3If – dog
cāseus, **cā**seī – 2m – cheese
cas**tel**lum, castellī – 2n – castle
cēna, **cē**nae – 1f – supper
cere**ā**lia, cere**ā**lium – 3n pl – cereal
cista, **cis**tae – 1f – box
clāvis, **clā**vis – 3If – key
crūs, **crū**ris – 3n – leg
crustulum, **crus**tulī – 2n – cookie

D

dēns, **den**tis – 3m – tooth
diēs, **di**ēī – 5m – day
digitus, **di**gitī – 2m – finger
dino**sau**rus, dino**sau**rī – 2m – dinosaur
discus, **dis**cī – 2m – disc
domus, **do**mī – irr f – home
dōnum, **dō**nī – 2n – gift
dracō, dra**cō**nis – 3m – dragon

E

ec**clē**sia, ec**clē**siae – 1f – church
ef**fi**giēs, effigi**ē**ī – 5f – statue
ele**phan**tus, ele**phan**tī – 2m – elephant
ēmptor, ēmp**tō**ris – 3m – buyer
eques, **e**quitis – 3m – knight
equus, **e**quī – 2m – horse
eruca, **e**rucae – 1f – caterpillar
escu**len**tum, escu**len**tī – 2n – tomato

F

faciēs, faci**ē**ī – 5f – face
fe**nes**tra, fe**nes**trae – 1f – window
ferculum, **fer**culī – 2n – tray
flōs, flōris – 3m – flower
folium, **fo**liī – 2n – leaf
fulmen, **ful**minis – 3n – lightning
fundus, **fun**dī – 2m – farm
furca, **fur**cae – 1f – fork
furnus, **fur**nī – 2m – oven

G

gēns, gentis – 3f – tribe
genū, **ge**nūs – 4n – knee
gigas, gi**gan**tis – 3m – giant
glaciēs, glaci**ē**ī – 5f – ice
grāmen, **grā**minis – 3n – grass
grex, gregis – 3m – flock
gryphus, **gry**phī – 2m – griffin

gutta, guttae – 1f – drop (of water)

H
harēna, harēnae – 1f – sand
herba, herbae – 1f – plant
hiems, hiemis – 3f – winter
holus, holeris – 3n – vegetable
hōrologium, hōrologiī – 2n – clock
hortus, hortī – 2m – garden

I
iānua, iānuae – 1f – door
iēntāculum, iēntāculī – 2n – breakfast
ignis, ignis – 3Im – fire
imber, imbris – 3m – rain
impedīmenta, impedīmentōrum – 2n pl – baggage
instrūmentum, instrūmentī – 2n – tool
īnsula, īnsulae – 1f – island
Iuppiter, Iovis – 3m irr – Jupiter
iūs, iūris – 3n – soup

K
Kalendae, Kalendārum – 1f pl – Kalends (the first day of the month)

L
lac, lactis – 3n – milk
lactūca, lactūcae – 1f – lettuce
lacus, lacūs – 4m – lake
lagoena, lagoenae – 1f – bottle
later, lateris – 3m – brick
lectus, lectī – 2m – bed
liber, librī – 2m – book
littera, litterae – 1f – letter
lītus, lītoris – 3n – shore
lūdus, lūdī – 2m – game
lūna, lūnae – 1f – moon

M
macellum, macellī – 2n – market

malleus, malleī – 2m – hammer
mālum, mālī – 2n – apple
manus, manūs – 4f – hand
mare, maris – 3In – sea
mōns, montis – 3m – mountain
mulier, mulieris – 3f – woman
mūs, mūris – 3m – mouse

N
nāsus, nāsī – 2m – nose
naufragium, naufragiī – 2n – shipwreck
nauta, nautae – 1m – sailor
nāvis, nāvis – 3If – boat
nix, nivis – 3f – snow
nōdus, nōdī – 2m – knot
nūbēs, nūbis – 3If – cloud
numerus, numerī – 2m – number
nummus, nummī – 2m – coin

O
oculus, oculī – 2m – eye
ōlla, ōllae – 1f – pot
ōrnāmentum, ōrnāmentī – 2m – ornament
ōs, ōris – 3n – mouth
ōsculum, ōsculī – 2n – kiss
ōstium, ōstiī – 2n – doorway
ovis, ovis – 3If – sheep

P
pānis, pānis – 3Im – bread
pāpiliō, pāpiliōnis – 3m – butterfly
pēs, pedis – 3m – foot
pila, pilae – 1f – ball
pirum, pirī – 2n – pear
pōculum, pōculī – 2n – cup
pōns, pontis – 3m – bridge
porcus, porcī – 2m – pig
prandium, prandiī – 2n – lunch
puella, puellae – 1f – girl
puer, puerī – 2m – boy, child
pupa, pupae – 1f – doll

Q

quārta **pars, quār**tae **par**tis – 1f 3f
  – one-fourth
quidnam!? – what on earth!?
quis**quil**iae, quisquili**ā**rum – 1f pl
  – garbage

R

raeda, **rae**dae – 1f – car
rāna, **rā**nae – 1f – frog
rēgīna, **rēgī**nae – 1f – queen
rēmigium, **rē**migiī – 2n – oar
rēte, **rē**tis – 3In – net
rēx, rēgis – 3m – king
rīsus, **rī**sūs – 4m – laughter
rixa, **ri**xae – 1f – big fight

S

saccus, **sac**cī – 2m – sack
sandal, **san**dalis – 3In – sandal
sarcina, **sar**cinae – 1f – backpack
scālae, scā**lā**rum – 1f pl – stairs
senex, **se**nis – 3Im – old man
sīmia, **sī**miae – 1f – monkey
sōl, sōlis – 3m – sun
solānum, solānī – 2n – potato
spe**ci**lia, spe**ci**lium – 3In pl – glasses

T

tabu**lā**tum, tabu**lā**tī – 2n – floor
taurus, **tau**rī – 2m – bull
tēle**phō**num, **tē**le**phō**nī – 2m –
  telephone

U

tempus, **tem**poris – 3n – time
the**ā**trum, the**ā**trī – 2n – theater
tractor, trac**tō**ris – 3m – tractor
tramen, **tra**minis – 3n – train
tuba, **tu**bae – 1f – horn
turris, **tur**ris – 3If – tower

U

um**bel**la, um**bel**lae – 1f – umbrella
umerum, **u**merī – 2n – shoulder
ursus, **ur**sī – 2m – bear
ūva, **ū**vae – 1f – grape

V

vēndor, **vēn**dōris – 3m – seller
ventus, **ven**tī – 2m – wind
vēr, vēris – 3n – spring
versi**pel**lis, versi**pel**lis – 3Im –
  werewolf
vespertiliō, vestpertili**ō**nis – 3m
  – bat
via, **vi**ae – 1f – road
vir, virī – 2m – man

X

xiphiās, **xi**phiae – 1m – swordfish

Y

nulla verba y littera incipiuntur

Z

zebra, zebrae – 1f – zebra
zōna, **zō**nae – 1f – belt

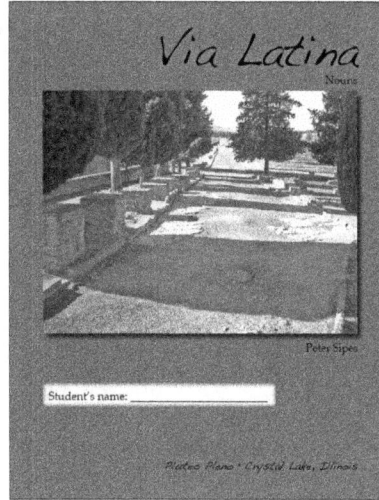

Primi Gradus in Latinitatem

Students often don't get the practice at connected reading in Latin that they should. Primi Gradus in Latinitatem is a series of readers designed to help students gain proficiency with Latin outside of a workbook and classroom setting.

Step 0: Words and simple stories

This step is aimed at the youngest students. They have never taken a Latin class, or maybe have learned a few simple things about Latin. Pictures will help guide students to meaning. Latin vocabulary is the focus of this step.

Step 1: Working with nouns

This step is aimed at students who are working through *Via Latina: Nouns*. Students at this level will still rely heavily on pictures for meaning. They might not have fully internalized Latin noun endings, and they may still take cues from standard word order.

Step 2: Working with verbs

This step is aimed at students who are working through *Via Latina: Verbs*. Students at this level should be independent readers in English. They should not need prompting with Latin nouns. Latin verbs are the focus.

Step 3: All parts of speech

This step is aimed at students who are working through *Via Latina: Parts of Speech*. Students at this level should have a good understanding Latin nouns and verbs. Latin's flexible word order shouldn't pose too many problems.

www.ingramcontent.com/pod-product-compliance
Lightning Source LLC
Chambersburg PA
CBHW071801020426
42331CB00008B/2356